WALKTHETALK.COM

Resources for Personal and Professional Success!

To order additional copies of this handbook, or for information on
other WALK THE TALK® products and services,
contact us at
1.888.822.9255
or visit our website at
www.walkthetalk.com

212°
the extra degree

Inquires regarding permission for use of the material contained in this book should be addressed to:

The WALK THE TALK Company
2925 LBJ Freeway, Suite 201
Dallas, TX 75234
972.243.8863

WALK THE TALK books may be published for educational, business, or sales promotion use.
WALK THE TALK® and WALK THE TALK® Company are registered trademarks of
Performance Systems Corporation.

Printed in the United States of America

10 9 8 7

Printed by MultiAd®

212°

for everyone

212°

212

At 211 degrees, water is hot.

At 212 degrees, it boils.

And with boiling water,
comes steam.

And with steam,
you can power a train.

One degree.

Applying one extra degree of temperature to water means the difference between something that is simply very hot and something that generates enough force to power a machine - a beautifully uncomplicated metaphor that ideally should feed our every endeavor - consistently pushing us to make the extra effort in every task, action and effort we undertake. Two-twelve serves as a forceful drill sergeant with its motivating and focused message while adhering to a scientific law - a natural law. It reminds us that seemingly small things can make tremendous differences. So simple is the analogy, that you can stop reading right now, walk away with the opening thought firmly planted in your mind and benefit from it for the rest of your life.

That's the purpose of this book - to help you internally define and **take ownership** of the most fundamental principle behind achieving life results beyond your expectations - a simple idea with a singular focus - an actionable focus.

Two-twelve.

It's this dramatic - three numbers joined together to form one, crystallizing a message that **absolutely assures** life altering positive results for those who choose to apply it.

212

Still looking for the "silver bullet" or "quick fix"
to achieving great results?

Stop.

Reams of material are written and taught with an approach to reaching an end by close to effortless means - and more will be written. Advertising messages continually promote methods of achieving end results with little or no effort. And this material and these messages are so effective that in many cases people will **work harder** to avoid the extra effort than actually applying the extra effort that will produce the originally desired outcome.

Great material with **solid** approaches to results have also been created and taught. Unfortunately, **action** on the part of the reader/ student in so many cases is the missing ingredient. And for those individuals who **do** take action, there are even a smaller number who make the **extra effort** necessary to reach the desired results that were originally set to achieve. Books are purchased, programs are attended and clubs are joined with wonderful intentions of putting forth the effort to achieve - only to end in another block of time invested half-heartedly with appropriately corresponding results. Why?

Why do you enter into any activity with anything but a
commitment to achieve your objective of that activity - not
a desire to achieve your objective, but a commitment?

212 is not only a message of action - it's a message of **persistent** and **additional action** - the continual application of **heat** (effort) to whatever task or activity you undertake in order to achieve not only the primary objective you seek, but to reap the **exponential** rewards that are possible by applying one extra degree of effort.

Illustrated in the following pages are examples and thoughts that should help you further understand and remind you of the exponentially different results that are possible by applying one extra degree of effort.

How many opportunities have you missed because you were not **aware** of the possibilities that would occur if you applied a small amount of effort beyond what you normally do?

People develop personal habits toward action and rarely attempt to develop them further and continually. Unless someone engages in frequent self-review or an external source (a friend, a book, a manager, a spouse, a parent, an article, etc.) brings something to one's attention - a person will continue throughout their lives making very small improvements if any at all.

Now you're aware of "212 - the extra degree". No longer will you be able to do only what is required of you and only what is **expected** of you. Because with awareness comes responsibility - to yourself and to others. And, again...

You are now **aware**.

The excitement can **begin**. Are you smiling yet?

You now have a **target** for everything you do.

212

You may not always be able to turn up the heat and hit the boiling point but that doesn't mean you shouldn't make the attempt. It's what you'd advise others to do and it's what we should teach our children.

211 can serve a purpose but 212 is the extra degree - the extra degree that will bring **exponential** results - exponential results to you and those you touch throughout your days.

You know there are no secrets to success. Success with anything, success **in** anything has one fundamental aspect - effort. To achieve exponential results requires **additional** effort. You know this (and if you didn't, you do now). Take your courses. Read your books. Listen to your tapes. But take action. Take action with commitment. Then, when you're ready for exponential results, apply the extra effort. Sometimes you'll have immediate exponential results and sometimes you'll realize the benefits of your extra effort much farther down the road. Regardless, in many cases, it may only be that one extra push that gets you ten times the results you were attempting to originally obtain. Pace your expectations and operate at your new target - two-twelve. You **will realize** the benefits of your extra effort.

At 211 degrees, water is hot.

At 212 degrees, it boils.

And with boiling water,
comes steam.

And with steam,
you can power a train.

It's your life.
You are responsible for your results.
It's time to turn up the **heat**.

From this day forward, **commit** to operating at 212 degrees in everything you do. Etch it into your thinking - into your being. Apply it to your actions. It guarantees to increase your results positively and in so many cases, increase your results exponentially.

212°

thoughts & facts

Inches make the champion.

Vince Lombardi
Hall of Fame football coach
1913 – 1970

Professional golf tournaments are comprised of four rounds (games) of 18 holes played over a four-day period (72 holes total). There are four major tournaments each year - The U.S. Open, The British Open, The PGA Championship and The Masters. The average margin of victory between 1982 and 2006 (25 years) in *all* tournaments combined was less than three strokes - less than a one stroke difference per day. From 2000 through 2006 (seven years), the winner across all tournaments took home an average of 77% more in prize dollars than the second place finisher (before endorsements and other dollars).

The Masters averages

Margin of victory in strokes (1982 – 2006)	2.28
Strokes per day	0.57
First place prize dollars (2000 – 2006)	$1,087,714
Second place prize dollars (2000 – 2006)	$652,629
Additional prize dollars for first place (2000 – 2006)	67%
Playoffs necessary to crown winner after 72 holes (1982 – 2006: 25 years)	6 (24%)

The U.S. Open averages

Margin of victory in strokes (1982 – 2006)	2.48
Strokes per day	0.62
First place prize dollars (2000 – 2006)	$1,042,857
Second place prize dollars (2000 – 2006)	$575,914
Additional prize dollars for first place (2000 – 2006)	81%
Playoffs necessary to crown winner after 72 holes (1982 – 2006: 25 years)	6 (24%)

The British Open averages

Margin of victory in strokes (1982 – 2006)	2.48
Strokes per day	0.62
First place prize dollars (2000 – 2006)	$1,112,092
Second place prize dollars (2000 – 2006)	$606,628
Additional prize dollars for first place (2000 – 2006)	83%
Playoffs necessary to crown winner after 72 holes (1982 – 2006: 25 years)	6 (24%)

The PGA Championship averages

Margin of victory in strokes (1982 – 2006)	2.20
Strokes per day	0.55
First place prize dollars (2000 – 2006)	$1,060,714
Second place prize dollars (2000 – 2006)	$600,057
Additional prize dollars for first place (2000 – 2006)	77%
Playoffs necessary to crown winner after 72 holes (1982 – 2006: 25 years)	6 (24%)

Many of life's failures are men who did not realize how close they were to success when they gave up.

Thomas Edison
American inventor
1847 – 1941

Courage is fear holding on
a minute longer.

George S. Patton
American soldier & general
1885 – 1945

Horse racing's classic races include The Kentucky Derby, The Preakness and The Belmont Stakes. A horse that wins each of these races in a single year is considered a Triple Crown winner - an unofficial title held by only 11 horses in the history of the sport. The Kentucky Derby and The Preakness last approximately two minutes with The Belmont finishing at just over two and a half minutes. The average margin of victory between 1997 and 2006 (10 years) over each of the Triple Crown races combined (30 races in all) was less than 3 lengths - 11 races were won by less than a length (37%). The average payout to the winner over all 30 races was nearly 450% more than the horse that placed second.

The Kentucky Derby averages (1997 – 2006)

Margin of victory in lengths	2.26
First place prize dollars	$1,655,820
Second place prize dollars	$216,000
Additional prize dollars for first place	667%

The Preakness (1997 – 2006)

Margin of victory in lengths	4.19
First place prize dollars	$628,815
Second place prize dollars	$195,020
Additional prize dollars for first place	222%

The Belmont Stakes (1997 – 2006)

Margin of victory in lengths	2.52
First place prize dollars	$583,260
Second place prize dollars	$194,420
Additional prize dollars for first place	200%

Triumph often is nearest when defeat seems inescapable.

B.C. Forbes
Founder & publisher
Forbes Magazine
1880 – 1954

The line between failure and success is so fine that we... are often on the line and do not know it. How many a man has thrown up his hands at a time when a little more effort, a little more patience, would have achieved success. A little more effort, and what seemed hopeless failure may turn to glorious success.

Elbert Hubbard
American writer & business person
1856 – 1915

The drops of rain make a hole
in the stone not by violence,
but by oft falling.

Lucretius
Roman philosopher
c. 50 bc -

At 33 degrees,
water falling from the sky on a Saturday is a rainy day.

At 32 degrees,
children are building snowmen, riding sleighs and
promising their parents that they're warm enough to stay
outside five minutes longer.

○

By making one extra mortgage payment a year,
a 30-year mortgage can be cut to 22.

○

It's the final steps of a journey that create an arrival.

Never stop.
One always stops as soon
as something is about
to happen.

Peter Brook
British theatre & film director
1925 –

Some men give up their designs
when they have almost reached the
goal; while others, on the contrary,
obtain a victory by exerting, at the
last moment, more vigorous
efforts than before.

Polybius
Greek statesman & historian
c. – 120 bc

Many Olympic event winners are chosen by a measure of time or distance. In most of these events, the margin of victory between winning the gold medal and no medal at all is extremely small.

During the 2006 Winter Olympic games, the margin of victory between a **gold medal** and no medal at all was…

Men's Giant Slalom	0.17 seconds
Women's Giant Slalom	1.15 seconds
Men's Two-Man Bobsleigh	0.36 seconds
Women's Two-Woman Bobsleigh	1.04 seconds
Men's 1000 Meter Speed Skating	0.44 seconds
Women's 1000 Meter Speed Skating	0.07 seconds

212°

During the 2004 Summer Olympic games, the margin of victory between a **gold medal** and no medal at all was…

Men's 200 Meter Freestyle (swimming)	0.62 seconds
Women's 200 Meter Freestyle (swimming)	0.43 seconds
Men's 800 Meter (running)	0.21 seconds
Women's 800 Meter (running)	0.06 seconds
Men's Long Jump	28 centimeters
Women's Long Jump	3 centimeters

You give 100 percent in the first
half of the game, and if that isn't
enough, in the second half
you give what's left.

Yogi Berra
Hall of Fame baseball player and manager
Holds the record for
the most World Series played and won
1925 –

Two of auto racing's premier events are The Daytona 500 (stock car) and the Indianapolis 500 (formula one). Each takes roughly three to three and half hours to complete. In the 10-year period between 1997 and 2006, combining all 20 races, the winner took the checkered flag by an average margin of 1.71 seconds and took home $1,426,003 in first place prize money. The average prize for the second place finisher was $716,464 - a difference of $709,539 - roughly half of the amount banked by the winner.

The Daytona 500 averages (1997 – 2006)

Margin of victory	0.175 seconds
First place prize dollars	$1,354,368
Second place prize dollars	$845,607
Additional prize dollars for first place	60%

The Indianapolis 500 averages (1997 – 2006)

Margin of victory	2.80 seconds
First place prize dollars	$1,497,639
Second place prize dollars	$587,321
Additional prize dollars for first place	155%

You may have to fight a battle
more than once to win it.

Margaret Thatcher
British Prime Minister
1925 –

And let us not be weary
in well doing; for in due season
we shall reap, if we faint not.

Galatians 6:9

212°

action

Ideas for implementing the 212 mindset in your life are suggested in the following pages. These are specific ways for you to begin taking 212 action **right now** - this week.

They're just the beginning for you. Grab hold of one or two and begin (or start with your own). Once you start, it'll be difficult for you to act in any other way. 212 will become a wonderful new habit in your world - a backdrop to all that you do - a habit that will create fantastic life results for you and help you serve as an influence to all those people around you.

Remember…

With awareness comes responsibility… responsibility to **act**.

As a friend

Choose to visit or talk with one extra friend each week and create 52 additional discussions among friends for the year.

Do something helpful and unexpected for one friend each week of the year and plant more than 50 additional possibilities of influence.

As a parent

Wake and act *each day* with the understanding that your actions will be absorbed by your children... and your children will grow to be contributing adults to the level of your influence.

Add an extra 15 minutes each day to the time you invest with your children - an equivalent of more than two weeks each year at work. Imagine the exponentially positive affect of investing two extra weeks each year exclusively in the development of your children.

As a spouse

Invest $100 each year in blank greeting cards and mail one each week to your spouse (at home or at the office) - more than 50 "love notes" are sure to create more than a few "love moments".

Allow your partner to have the last word in two "discussions" each week where you'd normally dig in your heels and add not only 100 events of kindness to your year, but probably an additional 10 years to both of your lives.

If your spouse is the one who normally has charge of the children on a daily basis, take over the role one extra day each month and add almost two weeks each year to his/ her personal time to recharge.

At work

Add a few hours each month to your professional development *outside* of the work day knowing that you'll have invested the equivalent of a full work week during the year in your most valuable asset... you.

Make the extra contact each day... a sales call... a customer... a brief discussion with a colleague... an encouraging talk with a member of your team. With contact comes opportunity. At the end of a year you'll have opened more than 200 additional doors of possibility.

As a manager

Act in accordance with the understanding that your management role has an objective of developing and encouraging others to succeed by doing the right tasks at the right time… every day… every week… every month… to become the best they can possibly be.

As a student

Invest an extra hour of study each week in the course that most interests you with the understanding that parts of it may become a piece of your life's work. At the end of the year, you'll have added the equivalent of one full workweek of dedicated study in your area of interest. This activity alone will put you far in front of the pack of those who do only what is required.

As a civic, church or business group member

Give a few extra hours each month to your organization's efforts so that at the end of the year, you've added a full workweek to its cause.

As a coach of a youth sports team

Plan your season and practices with the formal *objective* in mind of developing the children's personal and athletic skills in addition to "having fun". Help them make the best use of *their* time.

In general

When you're working out, complete an additional repetition in your exercise because you know the big results are driven by the final repetitions, not the first.

Eliminate one half hour of television watching each day and get 182.5 hours each year to allocate elsewhere (equivalent to four and half weeks at work).

212 reflections

These are additional ideas and thoughts to help you make 212 a part of your daily actions.

Add 10 minutes to your day.

Alarm goes off. Snooze button is hit.

The thought (if any at this hour)...
"Just 10 more minutes."

212 approach

Night before. Alarm is set 10 minutes earlier than usual.
Next morning. Alarm goes off.

The thought...
"Beautiful. 10 more minutes I can add to my day."

A small difference that adds the equivalent of over one and half work weeks to your year - to be used how you wish. What could you do with that extra time?

Push it to 20 minutes a day and you've just bought more time than most people get each year for a vacation.

212 commitment

Add 10 more minutes to every day.

This is your wake up call.

Indulge your good side.

You see the opportunity. You are aware.

But you're busy.

"I need to be somewhere, doing something, otherwise I'd help."

"Someone else will do it."

"Someone else will pick it up."

"Someone else can handle it."

"It's not my responsibility."

212 approach

A person struggles. You help. A door needs to be open.
You open it. A piece of trash is in your path. You pick it up
and throw it away. A child needs some extra attention. You
give it to them. A job needs to be completed. You do it.

Allowing one less opportunity of service or kindness fall to
the wayside due to laziness each week will add 52 acts of
inspiration to your year. Push it to two a week and you add
more than 100. Imagine the possibilities.

212 commitment

Indulge your good side once more each week.

Be 212. Start now.

Cease to complain.

The weather.
The traffic.
My boss.
My customer.
My mother.
My father.
My sister.
My brother.

I don't have enough… But I really need…

I can't… If only [he, she, they] would…

It's been a tough [day, week, month]…

It's [Monday, Tuesday, Wednesday, Thursday, Friday]…

212 approach

Be. Move forward. Cease to complain.

Your words move others. Your words move you. Make yours send everyone in the right direction.

Complaining once less a day chokes off 365 seeds of negativity a year.

212 commitment

Put a smile in the path of a complaint… once daily.

Cease to complain.

Be valuable. Encourage the principle.

You sit talking with someone - listening to the rationalizations, the excuses, the reasons why it's "okay" to do something or not do something you know to be against what is right or what is sound.

"After all, we're only human."
"We have to choose our battles."
"We can't fix everything."
"We don't want to upset anyone."

We let the rationalizing pass, the excuse for the lesser action taken with a supportive "that's true", "the most important thing is you tried" or some other affirmation of what we know to be false.

212 approach

You challenge the rationalization. You awaken someone to their excuse. You call them on the contradiction.

"Yes Men", "Yes Women" provide no value.

Be valuable to your family, friends and associates. Once more each week, avoid the simple path for its ease and create 52 more possibilities of "the right thing" being done each year.

212 commitment

Encourage the principle. Encourage the virtue. Encourage character. Once more each week.

Be valuable.

Pause and reflect.

You skim the material.

"Great stuff."

"Really makes sense."

"I like that a lot."

You move on.

Quickly.

212 approach

You read the material. You pause. You reflect. You give it thought. Deeper thought. You embrace it or toss it aside but you do so after pausing - after reflecting on it for more than an inattentive moment.

Thought is important because it is thought that generally precedes action.

Pausing and reflecting - investing thought beyond an instant twice more each week on a particular topic creates more than 100 additional possibilities of action and/ or improvement each year.

212 commitment

Pause and reflect - deeper - twice weekly.

Prune the diversions.

Prune. Not the fruit. The verb.

To prune a tree is to remove the branches and shoots that do not serve its growth and vigor.

But it goes one step further.

A diseased branch or low performing shoot not only does not serve the tree - it drains the energy that can be used elsewhere - the energy that can produce more fruit, more flowers and stronger branches.

When did you last evaluate the tasks you do every day against what's most important to you? When did you last evaluate them against who's most important to you? You have goals. You have time.

You have energy.

Where should it be invested?

212 thought

Removing just two diversions from your life each week eliminates more than 100 distractions from what's most important to you.

212 commitment

Prune the diversions. Twice weekly.

Risk. Attempt.

Comfort. Risk.

Both are enjoyable.

One we strive to create. One we try to minimize.

One can make us lazy. One can make us stronger.

When did you last risk failure? When did you last leave your comfort zone?

212 challenge

Step out of your comfort zone once more each week and create over 50 additional opportunities for excitement, challenge and possibility each year. This is what life's about.

212 commitment

Risk. Attempt. Fail. Succeed. Once more each week.

It's been said that youth is wasted on the young.

By taking risks, we assure life isn't wasted on the living.

Risk. Attempt.

Find the time. Give the time.

Time. Money.

Which is more valuable?

Lose them both.

Which can you get back?

In your efforts to be charitable, to contribute to your community, which do you more quickly give - your time or your money?

212 challenge

Go deeper into your pockets - past the paper, past the coins.

Find the time. Give the time.

Contribute two hours a week to your cause and/ or community and you'll be donating more than two and half work weeks a year of life's most valuable commodity: time.

212 commitment

Start a habit. Inspire a habit. Donate two hours of community contribution to the cause of your choice... weekly.

Find the time. Give the time.

afterword

212°

Involvement and reminders drive continual awareness. And with awareness comes responsibility and action.

Let the number 212 serve as your constant reminder. It's your new way of thinking - your new way of acting. Write it down and leave it wherever it might serve you best - wherever you may need a prompt to extra action (or just action itself)... your bathroom mirror... the dashboard of your car... in your "cube" at work... on your refrigerator... above the door of your workout room.

For 212 decals, mugs, t-shirts and other gear please visit **www.212club.com.** To license the 212 logo for use on company, team or organizational materials, please visit **www.212club.com/logo.**

To order additional copies of **212° the extra degree,** visit **www.walkthetalk.com**

It's time to turn up the **heat**. Go to work.

about the author

S. L. Parker is cofounder of MaxPitch Media, Inc. (www.maxpitch.com) - publisher of justsell.com, the Web's resource for sales leaders™. A native of the Washington, D.C., area, he now lives in Richmond, Virginia, with his wife, Jennifer (an artist), and their three children.

He can be reached with feedback or to discuss speaking engagements at **sam@justparker.com**. On the web, he continues to explore the details of life and business at **www.justparker.com**.

WALKTHETALK.COM

Resources for Personal and Professional Success!

about the publisher

Since 1977, The WALK THE TALK Company has helped
individuals acquire the skills and confidence they need to
be effective leaders...and helped organizations develop
cultures built on ethics, values, and superior performance.
The WTT Company offers a full range of proven resources
and customized services-all designed to help organizations
turn shared values like integrity, respect, responsibility,
customer service, trust, and commitment into
workplace realities.

10 ways to use 212° the extra degree

1. Use as a training and development resource.
2. Give copies to your employees, customers and friends as a special thank you.
3. Have a copy of 212 waiting on your team's desk when they arrive to work on Monday morning to encourage "the extra degree" of effort for the weeks and months moving forward.
4. Send copies of 212 out to your resellers and franchisees to remind them of the exceptional value derived from pushing it just a bit more.
5. Ready your team for a 212 theme for the rest of the year.
6. Find one or two people whom you enjoy and form a small 212 group that mentors and encourages each other to put forth "the extra degree" of effort in whatever it is you're involved.
7. Give copies out as gifts to your employees, customers and friends.
8. Present as a "first order" thank you gift.
9. License the material to produce a private-labeled version with a corporate or group note as the forward.
10. Offer as meeting or convention gift to reinforce your theme.

WALKTHETALK.COM

Have questions? Need assistance? *Call 1.888.822.9255*

☑ **Please send me more copies of 212° the extra degree™**

1-99 copies $9.95 each 100-499 copies $8.95 each 500+ copies, *please call*

212° the extra degree _____ copies x _____ = $ _____

Product Total	$	_____
*Shipping & Handling	$	_____
Subtotal	$	_____
Sales Tax:		
Texas Sales Tax—8.25%	$	_____
CA Sales/Use Tax	$	_____
Total (U.S. Dollars Only)	$	_____

*Sales & Use Tax Collected on
TX & CA Customers Only*

---

*Shipping and Handling Charges

No. of items	1-4	5-9	10-24	25-49	50-99	100-199	200+
Total Shipping	$6.75	$10.95	$17.95	$26.95	$48.95	$84.95	$89.95+$0.25/book

Call 972.243.8863 for quote if outside the continental U.S. • orders are shipped ground delivery 3-5 business days.
Next and 2nd business day delivery available—call 1.888.822.9255.

Name_____Title _____

Organization _____

Shipping Address (No P.O. Boxes) _____

City _____ State _____ Zip _____

E-mail _____ Phone: _____ Fax: _____

Charge Your Order ❏ MasterCard ❏ Visa ❏ American Express

Card Number _____Exp. Date _____

❏ Check Enclosed (payable to The WALK THE TALK Company)

❏ Please Invoice (Orders over $250 ONLY) ❏ P.O. Number (required) _____

See reverse side for additional ordering information.

Prices effective March 2007 are subject to change.

Four Easy Ways To Order

212° the extra degree™

ONLINE

walkthetalk.com
visit our website 24 hours a day

FAX

972.243.0815

MAIL

The WALK THE TALK® Company
2925 LBJ Freeway, Suite 201
Dallas, TX 75234

or

PHONE

1.888.822.9255 (Toll Free), or 972.243.8863
Monday through Friday, 8:30 a.m.—5 p.m., Central

WALKTHETALK.COM

Resources for Personal and Professional Success!